You are the one thi
when all the otl

(...you know like  stuff
or or stuff)
Suddenly buggers off without telling you
& leaves you RIGHT in the lurch.

You're that pint in the pub
that turns into a four-o-clock-in-the-
morning-what-happened-there.

You're that stupid dare
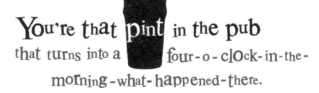
that-ends-up-in but-you're-jolly-lucky-there's
-no-permanent-damage.

You're cheering on the sidelines
in the pouring rain at the bi-annual
nowheres-ville fun-run kind of thing.

Yes…

Friend Ship,

it's there in your name isn't it…
You're a "friend", "Ship" (stay with me here)
Sailing the waters of life.
Through the storms & the high waves
you battle on.

And when the Skies are blue
there's no better place to be.

Mind you,
it's not always plain sailing…
I mean there was the time you
borrowed that DVD & never gave it back

for instance…

But the interesting thing is that
when it boils down to it,
no matter how much time passes,
we can just,
you know,
pick up where we left off.

Yes Friend ship,

you are what I want
most out of life.
I want you there
through the good times
& the slightly less good.

Friendship,
You rock.

(I still want the DVD back by the way.)

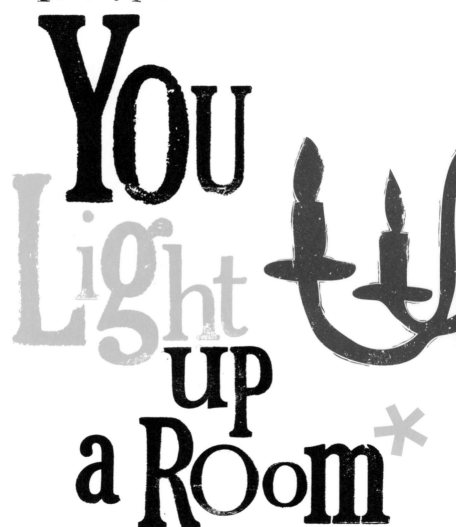

YOU, my friend...

YOU
Light up
up
a Room*

* In the Vibe
rather than
electrical sense.

And Because you are SO great, I am proposing a:

YOU APPRECIA

Membership rules:

1. All members must think you are Utterly brilliant. (Not hard.)

2. All members must regularly buy you presents & offer to make the tea.

3. No being grumpy.*

4. All members must wear a badge with your face on it at all times.

*Or mentioning the DVD you never gave back

...ION SOCIETY

Society activities:

1. Making your face badges

2. Talking about how **amazing** you are

3. Spending time with you

4. Thinking of ways to take the society global*

*We could call it Yourfaceisacebook
...What do you think?

Yes, I think...

The Best Present you can give is Friendship*

*Except for kittens.
Kittens also make a
really very
excellent present.

(Just throwing it out there.)

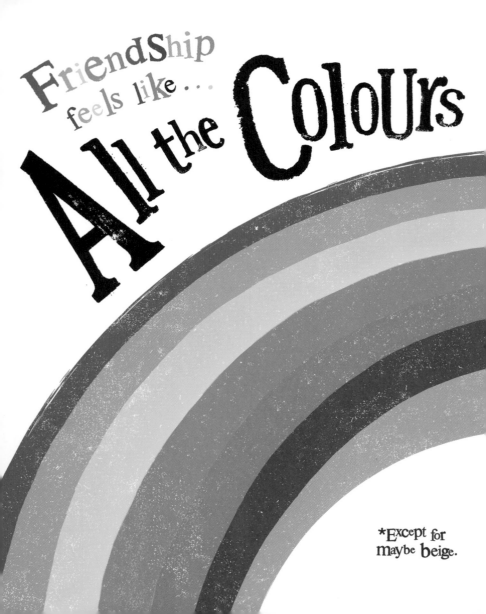

Friendship feels like...

All the ColoUrs

*Except for maybe beige.

And when you **Smile** the World Smiles with you*

*Unless you are being told Off for Something really
Very naughty indeed, when Smiling may result
in hand-to-face Contact

Fifteen Fabulous & F

Write a letter to somebody just because

PLAY more

Surprise someone with an impromptu cheeseboard

Whenever you find yourself waiting in line, strike up a conversation with the person next to you in a bid to make friends.

(Unless you are in an actual line-up, like an identification parade sort of thing.)

Throw Caution to the Wind & suggest a spontaneous soirée

Be the happy sort

Don't sweat the small stuff

(or the medium/big stuff)

Friendship Frolics

Ask for a bit of help now & again

Call Up a friend every day just to say hello

Change the World with Only love & friendship *and Cake

Laugh till your tummy hurts (medium to can't-take-it-anymore pain recommended)

Be generous* *especially to me

Dance around Something

Turn OFF the T.V. Turn ON the Charm

Get together as often as possible

reMember...

When
you're a true
friend & you do Something loVely,
It ripples through the UNiverse
(like a ripply thing)
more than you can possibly imagine.
So that One Nice thing
might even eventually reach,
I don't know,
Outer Mongolia
Or something.

Outer Mongolia

Complete & Utter

You are beyond **brilliant**

Sliced
bread
has
nothing
on you

You are
maximum
lovely

You
mean the
World to
me

Truenesses about you

You are humanified **Sunshine**

I'm the **most** **me** when I'm with **you***

You **always know** the **right** thing to **Say**

*Are you blushing yet?

The goOd friend's Mantra

I will keep in touch
& not forget to Call.
(This may require having it tattooed to
something but...well...whatever it takes.)

I will remember not just the
big important days like
birthdays & anniversaries,

but also the little things
that sometimes mean the most,
like the Scary dentist appointment
or a job interView or an
Oh-my-god-there's-no-Wine-in-
the-house type emergency.

Things like that.

And when sometimes my friends
forget that stuff
I'll be the sort of friend
that doesn't mind really.
(I really don't.)

And if I see something
& it makes me think of a person
I will get it or take a picture of it
& send it right there & then
for no other reason than
because it will make them go
"Oooh lovely."

I will never think
"I'm too busy, it can wait till tomorrow."*

*Tomorrow
never
comes.

I will be there when times are Good & there's chocolate aplenty.

I will also be there when times are rocky & there's not a chunk of chocolate in the house. (Will I? Really? Yes I will.)

I will be there in a crisis, in a drama, in celebration, & in ALL of life.

Yes,
I will try to be a good friend.
The One who comes up on speed dial.
The One who you can sit in silence with
& not even notice the silence at all.

I'll be the friend who tells you
if everyone can see your pants
or you've got Spinach
in your teeth
(which you don't by the way).

The One Who's there
no matter what.

I will do this for you,
because it's Only a tiny little bit
of what you do for me.*

* It really is.

Yes, a friend is the mOst Amazing Thing You can Have & Be*

*In particular when the friend I have is you & the friend I am is me.

I think what I'm really trying to say, in a roundabout way, is: YOU ARE AMAZING

More amazing than you will ever know.

THANK YOU (for being you).